To my beautiful boys, may you learn the art of self care and continue to find happiness in helping others. I am so proud of you and your kind souls.

One Goat Publishing

Bundjalung Country
Banora Point, NSW, Australia
www.onegoatpublishing.com

Text and illustrations copyright © Dannielle Pickford 2022

All rights reserved. No part of this book may be reproduced or used in any manner without written permission from the copyright owner.

For more information, contact onegoatpublishing@gmail.com

 A catalogue record for this work is available from the National Library of Australia

One Goat Publishing acknowledges the Traditional Owners of the country in which we live and work, the Bundjalung nation, and recognises their continuing connection to the land, waters. We pay our respects to the Elders - past and present and through them to all Australian Aboriginal and Torres Strait Islander people.

978-0-6451681-7-4 Paperback
978-0-6451681-8-1 Hardback

**HUDSON** was lots of things. He was brave, adventurous, loud, kind, and thoughtful. Most of all, Hudson was helpful.

**HUDSON** helped with lots of things.

Sometimes, Hudson was a little **TOO HELPFUL.**

Everyone knew they could rely on **HUDSON.**

One day, Hudson woke up and felt different. He didn't feel like being helpful today.

He didn't feel like doing anything. He just wanted everyone to **GO AWAY.**

At first, everyone was confused and even a little **CRANKY.**

They kept calling and calling and calling.

Hudson made himself a fort and hid inside.

Hudson had spent so much time helping others that he had forgotten to help **HIMSELF!**

His family tried to think of ways they could help Hudson feel like himself again.

First, **MUM** dropped in with his star light and some soft blankets.

'Getting **WARM AND CUDDLY** always makes me feel better,' said Mum.

Then DAD dropped by with a fruit platter.

'YUMMY FOOD always makes me feel better,' said Dad.

Next, **NAN** popped in with some books.

Lastly, Hudson's little brother **COOPER** crawled in with a teddy and snuggled in close.

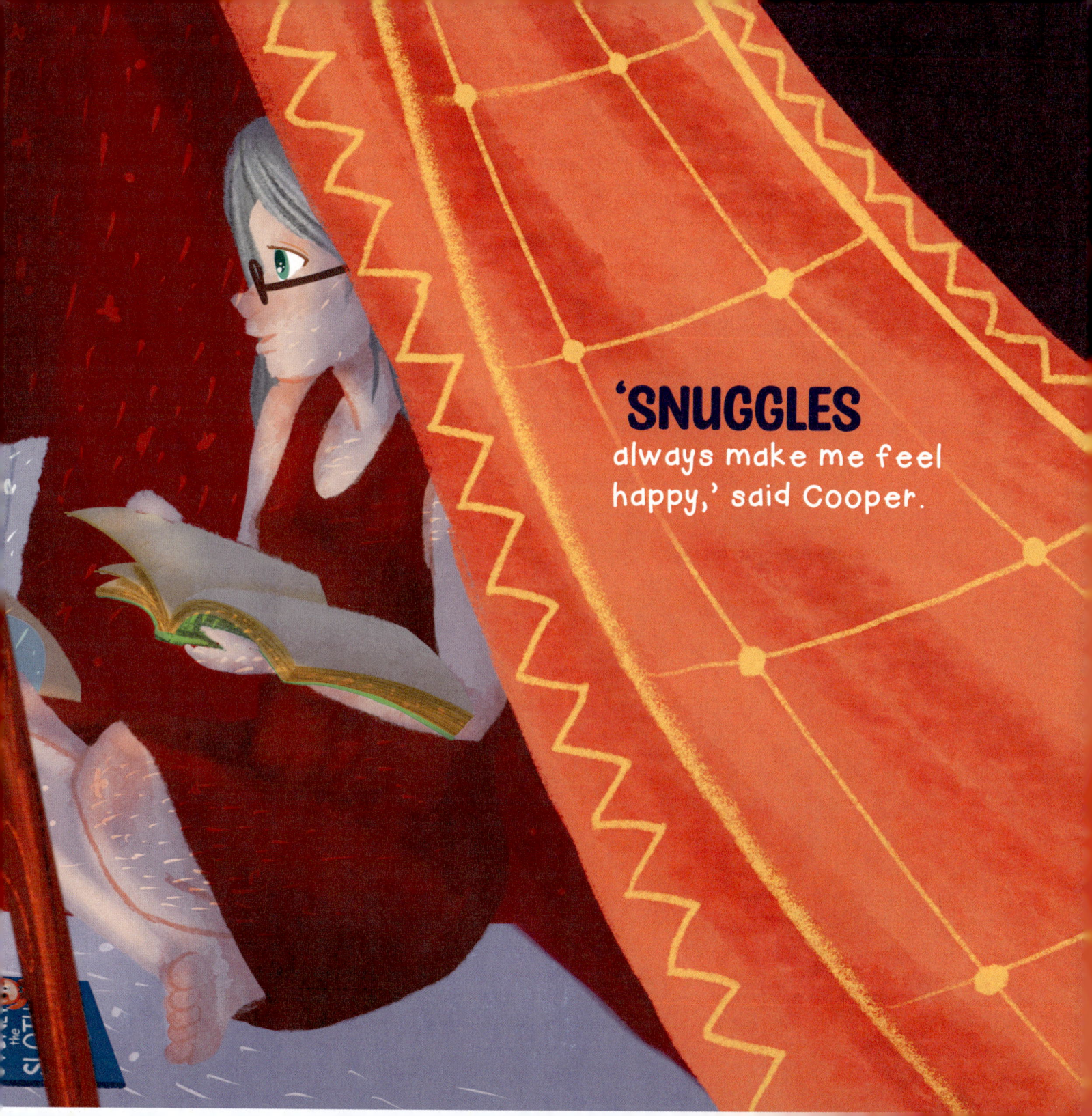

'SNUGGLES always make me feel happy,' said Cooper.

The next day, Hudson woke up feeling
**MUCH BETTER.**

Everyone was very grateful to have him back.
Hudson had learnt a **VALUABLE LESSON.**

In order to help others, Hudson needed to make sure he looked after himself too.

Luckily, Hudson now knew exactly how to help himself.

If you enjoyed this book
please consider leaving a review

You can find more books from Dannielle Pickford at
**onegoatpublishing.com**

Made in United States
Orlando, FL
20 June 2023

34355853R00020